DINOSAUR WORLD

BARDFIELD PRESS

First published in 2004 by Miles Kelly Publishing Ltd
Bardfield Centre, Great Bardfield, Essex, CM7 4SL

This edition published in 2006 by Bardfield Press
Bardfield Press is an imprint of Miles Kelly Publishing Ltd

2 4 6 8 10 9 7 5 3

Editorial Director:
Belinda Gallagher

Art Director:
Jo Brewer

Cover Designer:
Candice Bekir

Designer:
Debbie Meekcoms

Cartoons:
Mark Davis

Production:
Elizabeth Brunwin

ISBN 1-84236-393-X

Printed in China

British Library Cataloguing-in-Publication Data
A catalogue record for this book is available from the British Library

Reprographics: Anthony Cambray

www.mileskelly.net

Contents

Dinosaurs arrive

reptiles rule

Dinosaurs first walked the Earth almost 230 million years ago. They lived in what is now Argentina, in South America. They included Eoraptor and Herrarasaurus. Both these dinosaurs were slim, fast movers, able to stand almost upright and run on their two rear legs. Very few other animals could do this at this time.

THINK WE'RE A BIT EARLY?

WHAT'S FOR DINNER? I'M STARVING!

FRESH LIZARD - AGAIN.

GRR! GRR! YUM YUM!

GULP!

Early dinosaurs were probably meat eaters. They hunted small animals such as lizards and insects.

The first dinosaurs had legs beneath their bodies, not sticking out to the side like other reptiles. This meant they could run – fast! A long tail balanced the head and body, and the neck was long, allowing the head to move around and sniff out prey. Claws were sharp for grabbing food and large mouths were filled with pointed teeth to tear up prey.

Dinosaurs were not the first creatures on Earth. Many other kinds of animals lived before them, including different types of reptiles. Over millions of years one of these groups of reptiles probably changed very slowly, or evolved, into the first dinosaur.

Their lightweight bodies and long, strong legs meant they easily chased after their prey.

Getting bigger

dino monsters!

Some dinosaurs became larger and started to eat plants rather than animals. Plateosaurus was one of the first big plant-eating dinosaurs. It grew up to 8 metres long and lived 220 million years ago in what is now Europe. It could rear up on its back legs and used its long neck to reach food high off the ground.

SMALL IS BEST!

LOOK KID, IF YOU WANNA GROW BIG, EAT YOUR GREENS!

THESE NEW LEAVES ARE A BIT TOUGH...

MUNCH! MUNCH!

Plant-eating dinosaurs reached up into trees for food. Their size protected them from enemies.

Plant-eating dinosaurs had teeth that were suited to their diet. Edmontosaurus had rows of wide, sharp-ridged teeth in the sides of its mouth – perfect for chewing tough plant foods such as twigs and old leaves. Apatosaurus' teeth were long, thin and blunt. They worked like a rake to pull leaves off trees.

Early plant-eating dinosaurs did not eat fruit or grass – they hadn't appeared yet! They ate plants called horsetails, ferns, cycads and conifer trees.

TRY A DIFFERENT TREE!

ERM... EXCUSE ME!

One plant eater, Riojasaurus, was 10 metres long. It weighed one tonne – as much as a family car!

Biggest of all

supersize!

MOVE IT!

The true giants of the Age of Dinosaurs were the sauropods.

These vast dinosaurs had a small head, long neck, barrel-shaped body, long, tapering tail and four pillar-like legs. The biggest sauropods included Brachiosaurus, Mamenchisaurus, Barosaurus, Diplodocus and Argentinosaurus.

AAATCHOOO!

BANG!

OWW!

Sauropods swallowed pebbles. These helped to grind and mash up the food in their stomachs.

can you believe it?

Diplodocus is also known as 'old whip-tail'! It could swish its long tail so hard and fast that it made an enormous CRACK like a whip.

Sauropods probably had to eat constantly, at least 20 hours out of every 24-hour day! Their enormous bodies needed huge amounts of food to keep them supplied with energy. But because their mouths were small they had to eat and eat and eat!

I SAID YOU COULD HAVE A **SNACK!**

HE'S EATING MY **HOUSE!**

MUNCH! MUNCH! MUNCH!

The biggest sauropods, like Apatosaurus, weighed up to ten times more than the elephants of today.

The biggest meat-eating dinosaurs were the largest hunters ever. Different types lived during the Age of Dinosaurs. Allosaurus was from the middle of this time. One of the last hunters was also one of the largest – Tyrannosaurus rex. An earlier hunting dinosaur was even bigger – Giganotosaurus.

These predators (hunters) had massive mouths and long, sharp teeth. Their claws could slice and slash.

Meat-eating dinosaurs probably caught food in various ways. They might hide behind rocks and rush out to surprise a victim. They might chase after prey or plod steadily for a time to tire out their meal. Or they might feast on the bodies of dead dinosaurs.

Some meat-eating dinosaurs not only bit their prey, but also each other! fossils of several Tyrannosaurus had bite marks on the head.

Fast-moving meat eaters were well-equipped for hunting large plant-eating prey.

Looking for fossils

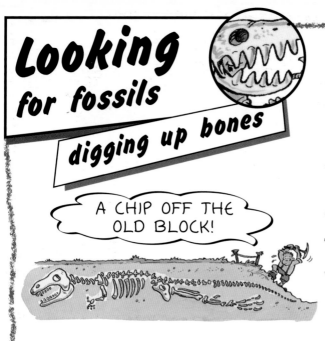

digging up bones

We know about dinosaurs because of fossils. These were once body parts, such as bones, claws and horns. They did not rot after death but were buried and preserved for millions of years. Gradually they turned to stone and became fossils, which give clues to how dinosaurs lived.

Palaeontologists are scientists who study dinosaur bones. They dig into rocks with hammers and picks.

Palaeontologists make notes and sketches and take photos to record every stage of a fossil 'dig'.

Finding all the fossils of a single dinosaur is very rare. Usually only a few are found, jumbled and broken.

Killer claws

or super slashers

Nearly all dinosaurs had claws on their fingers and toes. These claws were shaped for certain jobs in different dinosaurs. They were made from a tough substance called keratin – the same substance that your fingernails and toenails are made of.

Meat eaters had curved, sharp claws for stabbing prey. Baryonyx had thumb claws for hooking fish.

Did you know...

Giant sauropods had almost flat claws. Dinosaurs like Apatosaurus looked like they had toenails on their huge feet!

Deinonychus had huge hooked claws on its feet. These claws could kick out and flick down like a knife.

Look! Listen! Sniff!
dino senses

Like the reptiles of today, dinosaurs could see, hear and smell the world around them. In fact, all their senses were well-developed. We know this from fossils. Preserved fossil skulls have spaces for eyes, ears and nostrils and dinosaurs relied on these to survive.

Some dinosaurs, like Troodon, had big eyes. It could probably see well in the dark to hunt at night.

As well as having big eyes and good vision, Troodon also had a big brain. This indicates that it was probably one of the smartest dinosaurs.

Dinosaurs' nostrils were at the front of the snout. They used them to sniff out food and enemies.

Peaceful plant eaters

or spiky customers

Plant-eating dinosaurs were peaceful creatures – unless under attack from meat eaters. Some had sharp horns and spikes to protect themeselves. Others had beak-shaped mouths to help them bite through tough plant stems.

Triceratops, like all other dinosaur names, is Latin. When translated it means 'three horns on the face'. This dinosaur was 9 metres long and weighed about 5 tonnes – that's more than an African bull elephant. The frill around its neck made Triceratops look even more fearsome.

Euoplocephalus

Protoceratops

Euoplocephalus had bone studs set into thick skin on its back. Its bony tail could be swung at predator

Styracosaurus

Triceratops

As well as long spikes around its neck frill, Styracosaurus could run at speeds of 32 kilometres an hour!

Fast and slooooooow

on your marks...

Dinosaurs walked and ran at different speeds, according to their size and shape. Today, cheetahs and ostriches are slim with long legs and can run very fast. Elephants and hippos are massive heavyweights and plod slowly. Dinosaurs were similar. Some were big, heavy and slow. Others were slim, light and speedy.

Muttaburrasaurus was a huge dinosaur. It could probably gallop at a top speed of 15 kilometres an hour.

The huge sauropod dinosaurs such as Brachiosaurus and Diplodocus have left fossil footprints. These tell us that they probably lived in groups or herds. Each footprint is the size of of a chair seat! Hundreds of footprints found together showed that sauropods often walked long distances together.

Struthiomimus was an 'ostrich' dinosaur – it was similar to today's biggest flightless bird, the ostrich. Like the ostrich, it ran upright on strong legs. It also had a horny beak-shaped mouth for pecking food.

PUFF! PUFF! PANT! PANT!

GRR! QUICK! GRAB HIS TAIL AND TRIP HIM UP!

IN YOUR DREAMS!

Struthiomimus was super-fast. It could probably reach speeds of 70 kilometres an hour.

Dinosaur armour

living tanks!

Some dinosaurs had body defences against predators. These might be horns and spikes, or hard lumps of bone like armour plating. Most armoured dinosaurs were plant eaters. They had to defend themselves against big meat-eating dinosaurs such as Tyrannosaurus.

Fast-moving meat eaters used their powerful jaws, claws and teeth to attack their prey.

Triceratops had three large horns on its face and a bony frill around its neck. It looked a little bit like a rhinoceros does today. Its sharp horns could do a lot of damage to an enemy.

When scientists dug up fossils of Iguanodon, they found a bone shaped like a nose horn. Scientists now think the spike was a thumb-claw.

BRING IT ON, TOOTHY!

YEAH!

SHIVER! SHAKE! QUIVER!

Armoured dinosaurs, such as Triceratops, put up a fight with their horns, spikes and bony tails.

Eggs and nests
having a baby

Like most reptiles today, dinosaurs produced young by laying eggs. These hatched into baby dinosaurs that gradually grew into adults. Fossils have been found of eggs with dinosaurs still developing inside, as well as fossils of just-hatched baby dinosaurs.

Most dinosaurs laid their eggs in a nest or buried them in soil, and left them to hatch on their own.

The eggs hatched after a few weeks. The shells were leathery and bendy, like reptile eggs today.

Most baby dinosaurs found their own food. Very few parent dinosaurs cared for their young.

Dinosaur babies
and doting parents

Some dinosaur parents did care for their babies. Fossils of the dinosaur Maiasaura include nests, eggs, babies after hatching and broken shells. A few of these fossils were of broken, unhatched eggs, which looked as though they'd been squashed by babies that had already hatched.

When they hatched from their shells, the baby dinosaurs grew very quickly!

Hundreds of fossil Maiasaura nests have been found. The nests showed signs of being repaired year after year, which suggests the dinosaurs returned to the same to place to breed.

Baby dinosaurs grew five times faster than human babies! A baby Diplodocus weighed 30 kilograms when it hatched!

ROCK ROCK

WHAT A BORIN' MUM YOU ARE!

TWINKLE TWINKLE LITTLE STAR....

Maiasaura young couldn't leave the nest, so both parents brought plant food to the babies.

Dinosaur neighbours
in air and sea

All dinosaurs walked and ran on land, as far as we know. None could fly or swim. However, many other creatures that lived at the same time could fly or swim. Some were reptiles, like the dinosaurs.

Can you believe it?...

The dinosaur Leaellynasaura was named after the daughter of the scientists who found its fossils!

FISH SUPPER... AGAIN.

SPLISH SPLASH!

Ichthyosaurs were reptiles that lived in the sea. Reptiles called pterosaurs soared through the sky.

Placodus was a sea reptile. It crushed shellfish with its rounded teeth and ate the flesh.

The largest pterosaur was Pteranodon. It was as big as a small plane and able to soar and glide.

Jurassic disaster
end of the dinos

The dinosaurs died out 65 million years ago. There are fossils in rocks up to this time, but there are none after. What happened to wipe out the biggest and most successful animals the world has ever seen? Some scientists think that a meteorite, a giant lump of rock, may have smashed into Earth creating huge clouds of dust.

Can you believe it?

Many of the birds that appeared after the dinosaurs could not fly!

WHOOOOOOOOSSSHHHH

BLIMEY – WHO THREW THAT?

GOOD FOR A BARBECUE!

Clouds of dust would have blocked out heat and light from the Sun – disaster for the dinosaurs.

Volcanoes may have erupted, making clouds of dust and gas that could have choked the dinosaurs.

A new disease may have slowly killed the dinosaurs. Or mammals may have stolen their eggs.

Index